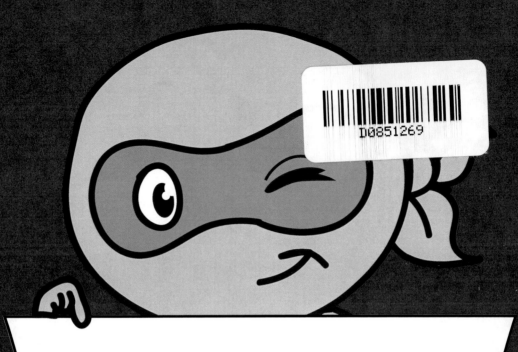

This book belongs to

_____

This book is dedicated to my children - Mikey, Kobe, and Jojo.
When someone else's happiness becomes your happiness, that is love.

Ninja Life Hacks™

Love Ninja

By Mary Nhin

Pictures By
Jelena Stupar

I love showering my family and friends with quality time, acts of service, and affection. I'm, also, not shy about saying "I love you."

Not long ago, I didn't know what love meant or how to show love. I thought love meant only kisses.

Love was icky...eeew!

So to find out, I went on a quest to look for the meaning of love.

The first house I stopped at was Compassionate Ninja's.

Then, I knocked on the house next door.

After leaving Stressed Ninja's home, I bumped into Shy Ninja.

All the interviewing made me hungry, so I walked to the nearest restaurant. While there, I ran into some ninjas so I decided to ask them, too.

Love is when you go out to eat and give somebody most of your French fries without making them give you any of theirs.

After lunch, I continued down the street. I walked a while until I got to Curious Ninja's house.

As I was leaving, I ran into Angry Ninja.
"Do you know what love means, Angry Ninja?"

I thought about what I had learned. There were so many ways to show love, and it didn't just mean kissing!

Then, I bumped into Lonely Ninja.

Remembering all the different ways to love could be your secret weapon in showing your loved ones you care.

Please visit us at ninjalifehacks.tv for box sets and fun, free printables.

[Instagram] @marynhin   @GrowGrit
#NinjaLifeHacks

[Facebook] Mary Nhin   Ninja Life Hacks

[YouTube] Ninja Life Hacks

Credit to *The Five Love Languages* by Gary Chapman